National Learning Association Everything You Should Know About: AMAZING ALASKA Faster Learning Facts

By: Anne Richards

All Rights Reserved. No part of this publication may be reproduced in any form or by any means, including scanning, photocopying, or otherwise without prior written permission of the copyright holder. Copyright © 2017

WHERE IS ALASKA?

The State of Alaska is situated in the extreme northwest of North America. It is bordered by the Canadian regions of British Columbia to the east and by Attu Island to its extreme West; the State also shares a marine border with Russia across the Bering Strait. To the North of Alaska are the southern parts of the Arctic Ocean, and the Pacific Ocean lies to the south. Alaska is the largest State in the United States but the most sparsely populated. Half of the residents of the entire State live in Anchorage which is Alaska's largest city but not its capital; the State Capital of Alaska is Juneau.

WHY IS ALASKA OFTEN KNOWN AS "THE LAST WILDERNESS?"

Alaska is often known as "The Last Wilderness" and with good reason; this absolutely stunning state is renowned for its colossal size, wide open spaces and mostly untouched natural scenic beauty. Alaska contains more land than the next three largest states combined, and boasts the highest mountain in North America, Denali which is 6,190 metres tall. There are more than 3,000 rivers and 3 million lakes in Alaska, and its largest lake, Lake Iliamna, is about the size as the State of Connecticut. Alaska also boasts Kodiak Island which is the largest island in North America and the largest temperate, intact rainforest in the world.

HOW DO ALASKANS TRAVEL?

We have established that Alaska is a massive land mass and that there is no shortage of lakes, rivers and natural beauty, but one thing this State does lack is major roads and highways. So much of the state is unsettled, and uninhabitable that for the most part major infrastructure for travel is not warranted. People in Alaska use different forms of travel such as riverboats, snow mobiles, dog sleds and railways, but one of the most popular forms of travel in Alaska is plane. Alaskans fly and own more aircraft than any other country in the world, and have eight times as many pilots as any other state in America.

WHO ARE THE NATIVE ALASKANS?

Before the arrival of Europeans to Alaska numerous indigenous people lived in the area for many thousands of years. One of the most prolific of these Native American Indian tribes were the Tlingit people who were a seafaring people who lived in southeast Alaska and the Yukon. Also located in the southeast of Alaska were the Haida tribe, renowned for their unique art. In 1887 President Grover Cleveland granted permission for the Tsimshian people to come to Alaska from British Columbia, and to settle on Annette Island and found the town of Metlakatla. Although many Native Alaskans died as a result of smallpox introduced by Europeans, many descendants of these tribes still exist as well as the Aleut people and other Native American Indian tribes such as the Athabaskans, the Eyak and various Inuit tribes that can still be found in the State.

WHEN DID THE UNITED STATES OF AMERICA BUY ALASKA?

The first Europeans arrived in Alaska in 1741 when Danish explorer Vitus Jonassen Bering spotted it on a voyage from Siberia in Russia. The first settlers in the area were Russian whalers and fur traders who established themselves on Kodiak Island in Alaska in 1784. The United States of America Secretary of State William H. Seward offered Russia 7,200,000 dollars for Alaska in 1867 which Russia accepted. On 18th of October 1867 Alaska officially became the property of the United States; at the time many Americans thought that the purchase of Alaska was a mistake and it became known as "Seward's Folly." It was not until 1959 that Alaska officially became the 49th state of the United States of America.

WHAT IS THE AURORA BOREALIS?

The stunningly beautiful Aurora borealis, better known as the Northern Lights can be seen from the town of Fairbanks in Alaska an average of 243 days a year, weather permitting. The Aurora borealis is an incredible natural light show in the sky that is caused by collisions between electrically charged particles. Fairbanks is large city in the Interior region of Alaska and has an estimated population of over 100,000 people. Fairbanks is also officially the coldest city in

America and has a winter average of −26.1 to −31.7 degrees Celsius.

HOW MANY ACRES DOES DENALI NATIONAL PARK COVER?

Denali National Park covers an astonishing six million acres of land. It is an incredibly breath taking untamed wilderness that is visited by 400,000 visitors a year who only get to see a comparably small part of this incredible natural wonderland. The park is home to lofty mountains and their snow-capped peaks, and well as forests, lakes, rivers and tundra. There is an incredible abundance of wildlife in the park which includes foxes, bears, wolves, caribou, and Arctic ground squirrels. Denali Park is of course also home to the record breaking Denali Mountain which was once known as Mount McKinley.

WHERE IS THE ALASKA VETERAN'S MEMORIAL?

The Alaska Veteran's Memorial is an outdoor memorial located within Denali State Park and consists of five concrete panels that are nearly 7 metres tall each. Each panel represents a different section of the armed services such as the Army, Air Force, Navy, Marines and Coast Guard, and are laid out in a crescent shape. On these panels is carved a brief history of the particular sector of the armed forces represented. There are also two impressive sculptures of territorial guards at the entrance of the memorial. The memorial also contains smaller monuments to the victims of plane crashes in the country, and to Alaskans who have been awarded the prestigious Medal of Honour.

WHAT TWO HUGE SPECIES OF BEAR CALL ALASKA THEIR HOME?

Alaska is home to the two largest breeds of bear in the world, the Kodiak bear and the Polar Bear. The Kodiak bear which is sometimes known as the Alaskan brown bear lives on Kodiak Island. These huge bears can grow in excess of 600 kilograms and be as tall as 2.44 metres when they stand of their hind legs. Polar bears are the largest meat eater that lives on the land and can weigh up to 680 kilograms. The Polar bears' diet mostly consists of seals and they spend much of their time at sea hunting.

WHAT IS THE STATE BIRD OF ALASKA?

The State bird of Alaska is the willow ptarmigan which is a rather large bird about the same size as a small chicken. They are brown and white in colour, but turn completely white in the winter. These birds are also found in Britain where they are known as red grouse, the British species does not turn white like its Alaskan counterpart. Willow ptarmigan mostly eat plant leaves and shoots as well as berries, seeds and insects; they inhabit tundra, open forests and shrub meadows high in the mountains where the temperature is colder.

WHAT FOOD DO PEOPLE EAT IN ALASKA?

As you might expect from a State with so much nature to hand, it is full of healthy wholesome food, and the Alaskans are particularly proud of their salmon which is exported and eaten worldwide. Apart from enjoying the abundance of seafood the country has to offer such as prawns, crabs, clams, mussels, and oysters Alaskans are also fond of their meat. Reindeer dogs are a popular Alaskan street food and are made just like hot dogs but with reindeer sausages. If you have a sweet tooth and are looking for a tasty desert to follow your reindeer dog then don't bother with the Eskimo ice cream or Agutuk to give it its correct name because it is about as far removed from ice cream as you can possibly imagine and is made from seal oil, reindeer, snow, animal fat and berries, and tastes absolutely vile!

WHAT IS DOG MUSHING?

Dog mushing is the official state sport of Alaska and a part of life that is very important in this enormous state. Dog mushing is when a team of dogs are harnessed to pull sleighs and other vehicles over usually snowy terrain. Dog mushing was practiced in Alaska long before the arrival of the first Europeans and is still a necessary mode of transport in many parts of the State. Dog teams are often used by rural residents who rely on them to hunt and travel, as well as people who practice dog mushing as a hobby. Dog mushing is also a very popular competitive sport and races are held between dog handlers and their teams all over the State.

WHEN WAS THE HAMMER MUSEUM OPENED?

The Hammer Museum in based in Haines, Alaska, and has more than 1,400 items on display some of which date back to Roman times. The Hammer Museum is recognisable because of the very large hammer that stands outside it. The museum was opened in 2001 by Dave Pahl who is a collector and restorer of tools. When Pahl moved to Alaska he became a blacksmith and taught himself the trade and started collecting tools. Pahl then purchased the 100-

year-old building in which he housed his collection and his museum was born. All this is not as crazy as it sounds and the world famous Smithsonian Institution was so impressed by this quirky museum that they go to Pahl for information on all things regarding tools, and in turn gave him a gift of five ancient tools for his collection.

WHAT IS THE FUR RONDY FESTIVAL?

Fur Rondy is Alaska's oldest and largest festivals, and is held every year in Anchorage in March. The event started in 1935 as a three day sporting event for miners and trappers; it originally featured hockey, skiing, boxing and a children's sled dog race. These days the events at Fur Rondy are a bit zanier, and outrunning reindeer and the downhill outhouse (outdoor toilet) race have also become popular features. The full name of the festival is the

Anchorage Fur Rendezvous, but was abbreviated by the locals. The Fur Rondy is also famous for its World Championship Sled Dog Races, in which mushers compete in three high-speed races over three days.

WHERE IS TRACY ARM LOCATED?

Tracy Arm is a spectacular fjord that is edged by glaciers, and is located south of the State Capital, Juneau. This stunning natural phenomenon is a popular destination for cruise ships and boat tours, and is named after Benjamin Franklin Tracy who was the Secretary of the Navy in the late 19th century. Tracy Arm is surrounded by sharp icy rock walls, glaciers, icebergs and waterfalls, and is situated in the Tongass National Forest. Tours of the fjord are hugely popular and it is not uncommon to see moose, bear and whales on a trip to this truly stunning location.

HOW LONG IS THE ALASKA HIGHWAY?

As we have already mentioned there are very few major roads in Alaska and this can make travel somewhat of a challenge, but in 1942 the Alaska Highway was built. The Alaska Highway runs from Dawson Creek in British Columbia in Canada through the Yukon Territory to Fairbanks. The highway was built for military purposes during World War II and was completed in a record time of eight months. This route is the most important means of access by land to the Yukon Territory and southern Alaska, and is a favourite with holiday makers. Lined with shops, restaurants, motels, hotels, and gas stations at 80 kilometre intervals the Alaska Highway is an incredible 2,237 kilometres long.

HOW OLD IS THE MOUNT ROBERTS TRAMWAY?

The Mount Roberts Tramway is the only tramway in southeast Alaska and opened to the public in 1996. The tramway operates from the month of May through to September and is located just south of downtown Juno. The Mount Roberts Tramway is one of the most popular tourist stops in southeast Alaska's and this system of cable cars carries 200,000 visitors each year. Cars rise nearly 550 metres into the air and offer views of downtown Juneau before travelling through a rainforest and onto Mountain House, where there are more amazing views of Juneau and the Gastineau Channel which is a channel between the mainland of the United and Douglas Island in the Alexander Archipelago of southeast Alaska.

WHO WAS JOSEPH JUNEAU?

Joseph Juneau was born in Canada in 1836 and was a miner and prospector. Along with another prospector, Richard Harris, he founded the city of Juneau now the state capital of Alaska. Juneau, Harris and their Native American guide Chief Kowee are credited with the first major discovery of gold in Juneau which lead to led to the Alaskan gold rush of 1880. The settlement founded by Juneau and Harris was originally called Harrisburg, but it is said that Joe

Juneau bought drinks for fellow miners to persuade them to name the city in his honour. Juneau and has been the State Capital of Alaska since 1900.

WHAT IS THE KENNECOTT MINES NATIONAL HISTORIC LANDMARK?

The Wrangell-St. Elias National Park is the largest and arguably one of the most stunning of Alaska's enormous national parks. Wrangell-St. Elias National Park boasts an incredible 16 of the highest mountain peaks in the United States of America. This majestic, mountainous region which borders the Canadian frontier is home to a vast array of wildlife and flora as well as glaciers and lakes. The park is a climbers paradise and equally as popular with walkers. The Kennecott Mines National Historic Landmark is an abandoned mining camp in the park that gives an insight into what life might have been like for early settlers and miners.

HOW LONG IS THE ALASKAN RAILWAY?

The Alaskan Railway runs through some of Alaska's most stunning country and connects stops like Anchorage, Denali National Parks and Fairbanks all through the summer months and at the weekends during the winter months. Unlike any other railway in the United States the Alaskan Railway carries both freight and passengers throughout its route. The railroad, including branch lines is 800 kilometres long and is owned by the State of Alaska. Construction on the Alaska Railroad began in 1903 near the town of Seward which is at the tip of the Kenai Peninsula, but the company building went into receivership after laying only 82 kilometres of track. In 1909 another private company managed to add another 34 kilometres of track before going bust; in the end the United States government under the Presidency of William Howard Taft completed the line.

Thank you! Thank you! Thank you!

It means a lot to us that you chose our book to spend your time learning with - we hope you enjoyed it!

All pictures and words were put together, with love, by experts from around the globe. Experts who love what they do and want to improve and educate the world, one book at a time!

We would really appreciate it if you could PLEASE take a second to let us know how we're doing by leaving a review on Amazon.

To leave feedback, Simply visit:

US Customers: https://amazon.com/feedback
UK Customers: https://amazon.co.uk/feedback

For all other customers, you can visit the "Your Orders" link from your Amazon menu and choose "Leave Seller Feedback".

Any comments you may have - what you enjoyed, any suggestions you might have and what you would like to read about in future books.

Any comments will help us understand better what you and your children most enjoy - this allows us to tailor future books and provide exactly what is most helpful and useful in the future.

National Learning Association

Made in the USA
Monee, IL
18 December 2019